Just a Thought

Inpirational thoughts,
scriptures and poems

Joy Hedges

CWR

All royalties from the sales of this book will be donated to Tearfund, at the request of the author. Tearfund is a Christian charity, working with local churches in poor countries to bring practical and spiritual help.

Acknowledgements

To God be the glory! Great things He hath done!
Frances van Alstyne (1820–1915)

I am so very grateful to the following people:

My parents, Rev Roderick H. Foster and Mary (née Battershill) for the good things they taught me, and their faith that ultimately I would get a book published!

My uncle, Dr David Foster, and his wife Dorothy for their prayers over twenty-four years that I would have a personal relationship with Jesus. This happened when I was sixty-four;

The late Dr Angus MacVicar, Scottish minister's son and prolific author, who urged the compilation of this book when I visited him in his Kintyre home three months before he died, aged ninety-three. Thanks to his encouragement of my writing over many years, I had chosen him as my godfather at the time of my confirmation;

The late Miss Isabel Henderson, blind poet and author of Christian meditation books, for her prayers and encouragement of my poetry, and becoming my godmother at the time of my confirmation;

The late Laura E. Salt, Children's Reference Book

Editor at Clarendon Press, Oxford (now OUP), who trained me from 1964–1966 to write and proof-read;

Lord Carey of Clifton for playing a major part in restoring my Christian faith, and for his kind permission to tell this story (see p.10). Following the Unity Service in Winchester Cathedral held on 24 January 2010, he called me 'a true missionary';

The late Rev Dr Selwyn Hughes for his friendship, books and inspiring Bible-reading notes, *Every Day with Jesus*;

Mary Payne, erstwhile editor of the Winchester *NewsEXTRA*, for enabling my articles to be published in her paper and offered online to 212 UK newspapers;

The Rt Rev John Perry, formerly Bishop of Southampton and Chelmsford, for his generous Foreword;

The conductors of many choirs who have perpetuated my love of singing and religious music;

Lynette Brooks, Sue Wavre, Rebecca Browne and other staff at CWR for their help and enthusiasm over this book;

Last but not least, the numerous friends, family and members of the medical profession who have encouraged, prayed and assisted me through untold struggles and obstacles encountered on my Christian journey.

Joy Hedges
December 2010

Contents

Foreword

J OY Hedges has a delightful way of relating a
Christian theme and truth to the everyday issues that
people face.

Her illustrations serve to bring home the practicalities
of a faith in God for daily living, and I am thankful
that some of her articles which have appeared in the
Winchester and Eastleigh *NewsEXTRA* are now available
in this book for wider readership.

Just a Thought reflects the author's own journey
of faith over the years. As a result it has a ring of
authenticity throughout, and I believe it will be a
great encouragement and inspiration to others. Her
understanding and experience of God touches the
deepest needs and hopes of the human heart, and I pray
that all who read this book will be blessed by it.

The Right Reverend John Perry
Formerly Bishop of Southampton and Chelmsford
July 2001

Preface: Through locked doors

Here I am to worship, here I am to bow down …
You're altogether lovely, altogether worthy …[1]

SO we sang at the fortieth anniversary celebrations of
Selwyn Hughes' Bible-reading guide, *Every Day with
Jesus*, at Waverley Abbey House in September 2005.

The Rev Dr Selwyn Hughes founded Crusade for World
Revival (CWR) prior to 1983, the year when Waverley
Abbey House was purchased. When interviewed by Chief
Executive Mick Brooks, Selwyn described how often God
gives us a vision which seems to prosper; then it dies and
is followed by a dreadfully barren experience; but if we
relinquish our own desire for glory and give it all to Him,
then He will resurrect us in a truly wonderful way.

This I found to be true in my own experience. In
December 2000, after nineteen years of trying to get
my Christian stories published, the opportunity came
to write a fortnightly column in the *NewsEXTRA*, a free
newspaper which covered Winchester (my home from
1990–2011), Eastleigh and Bishops Waltham, reaching
62,000 households. I wrote more for non-believers, as I
myself had not come fully to faith until the age of forty,
and was well aware of the remarkable change God had
subsequently made in my life.

At secretarial college our English tutor said to me: 'You're not to be a secretary but a journalist!' I then had little confidence, and funked it; consequently having to endure many unsuitable jobs. But the Lord was forgiving and gracious in opening this hitherto locked door when I was fifty-seven. He brought masses of ideas to mind, and the Holy Spirit produced suitable Bible quotes for each one! The task was a tremendous privilege and challenge, thoroughly enjoyable and a dream come true. The articles in this book are a selection from those published in the *NewsEXTRA* by my supportive editor, Mary Payne, between 2000 and 2004.

In *Every Day with Jesus,* Selwyn Hughes wrote: '… one of the ways in which God helps us to deepen our roots – He permits trials and troubles to come to us so that we might find solace and comfort in Him.'

A prayer: Dear Lord, please grant strength in my weakness, belief when I doubt and perseverance against *all* odds stacked against me. Amen.

Joy Hedges
Winchester, 2 February 2010

---

1. Extract taken from the song 'Here I am to Worship' by Tim Hughes. Copyright © 2000 Thankyou Music. Used by permission*

1.
Every one of us matters to God

'**R**EMEMBER Christ chose Zacchaeus, Mary Magdalene and the boy with the picnic,' said Archbishop Robert Runcie, looking straight into my soul.

I had just been interviewing him for a local and some Christian newspapers after he preached a sermon stating 'People Matter' at a theological college in Bristol where I worked as a lowly secretary. Dr George Carey, who was destined to succeed Dr Runcie, then became principal. Although I left my post before George's appointment, both he and his wife Eileen have remained friends ever since.

In 1982, George invited me to his induction service in Bristol Cathedral and to the students' Christmas carol service. At the carol service they enacted a scene set in the Shepherds' Fields near Bethlehem, which my father and I had visited the previous spring. The choir sang Bach's famous chorale 'O Sacred Head Once Wounded', which I had sung several times when a member of the London Philharmonic Choir.

At the age of fourteen I had made a decision to follow Christ, and at seventeen officially became a member of Father's Methodist church in Bideford, North Devon. But when working in London in 1962, worldly snares led me first to agnosticism and then to atheism. George's kindness helped me realise the pain I had caused Jesus in running away from Him for twenty-one years. At the carol service, tears poured down my cheeks. My friend beside me whispered, 'He's really talking to you, isn't He?' She and her boyfriend had been praying daily for my return to faith.

A week later, I was singing during the carol service at my local church when suddenly I felt the presence of Jesus both in my head and heart. I perceived He was not only alive, but also had saved a sinner like me from going to hell. Afterwards I told the vicar of this revelation and asked to be confirmed. The service took place the following March, attended by ten family members and even some non-Christian friends. The church librarian gave me a copy of Selwyn Hughes' devotional *Every Day with Jesus*, which has wisely guided my Bible reading ever since.

A year after conversion I was finally baptised by full immersion at Bathford Baptist Chapel, Avon.

This entire experience was the turning point in my often difficult journey towards God.

If a man owns a hundred sheep, and one of them wanders away, will he not leave the ninety-nine on the hills and go to look for the one that wandered off?

Matthew 18:12

Use me, O God

O Lord, let me be used by You:
May Your light shine through;
No one cares as You do;
None has a heart so true.

You were abandoned – so it seemed –
Upon the cross which us redeemed
From the dark sin to which we clung;
You willingly bleeding hung
Till we were cleansed by Your death,
And loved with every fleeting breath.

You wore a crown of thorns which tore
Your brow, as our harsh words cut sore
Into each other's minds. So we
Man's godliness can fail to see.

But Father God was near His Son –
His only beloved One –
In all the loneliness and grief.
Your suffering was great but brief
Because You rose on Easter Day,
And still triumphant lead the way.

2.
A dream come true for Father

I'M thankful I took my father on a surprise trip to Israel in April 1982. He was seventy-three, and died three months later.

The first morning, we climbed the flat roof of our hotel with a panoramic view of the Holy City. 'Jerusalem! I never thought I'd see it,' Father exclaimed. This had been his lifelong dream, of which I was unaware.

My favourite place was the church of Dominus Flavit ('the Lord wept'), recalling Jesus' agonising over the future sacking of Jerusalem by the Romans in AD 70. We visited the harrowing Holocaust Museum where we saw photographs of pile upon pile of children's shoes, and the eternal flame in remembrance of those arrested young lives. Our excellent guide was a Graeco–Jew, liberated from Auschwitz, where both his parents and brother had died.

A coach took us to Megiddo, where twenty layers of civilisation and the remains of Solomon's stables had been excavated. The terrain was uneven, and I suggested my father might prefer to stay on the coach because of his arthritic knee. 'I'm not going to miss a thing,' he replied. His favourite site was the fields near Lake Galilee where the miraculous feeding of the 5,000 occurred, 'Because this remains just as it was in Christ's day'.

We swam in the lake, which was like a warm bath, the air temperature being about eighty-five degrees Fahrenheit. And we took a boat from Tiberias to Capernaum to see the ruined synagogue where Jesus preached from Isaiah 6 the prophecy of His own coming.

One supposed site of Christ's tomb is the ornate church of the Holy Sepulchre, just outside Jerusalem's city wall; but we preferred the Garden Tomb below the Place of the Skull, where the body of Jesus was laid on that first Good Friday and from where He rose again on Easter Sunday.

'He is not here; he has risen, just as he said.'
Matthew 28:6

3.
A father's forgiveness

A TRUE modern version of Jesus' parable of the prodigal son is movingly told in *The Father Heart of God* by Floyd McClung.[1]

Sawat left his Christian home in a Thai village to seek excitement in Bangkok. He was shocked to find that the top floors of most hotels were used by prostitutes – some as young as nine – and learnt that more than ten per cent of all Thailand's girls ended up in the sex trade.

Unfortunately, Sawat got sucked into this evil. He sold opium, propositioned tourists and even helped buy and sell very young prostitutes. He became a popular major figure in the business.

Then he was robbed and arrested, and the underworld believed he was a police spy. In ignominy, he lived in a shanty beside the city rubbish dump.

When Sawat had left home for the city his father had said, 'I am waiting for you.' Sawat now wrote to him: 'I want to come home, but I don't know if you will receive me. I have sinned greatly, Father. Please forgive me. Next Saturday I will be on the train which stops at our village.

If you are still waiting for me, will you tie a piece of white cloth on our po tree?'

On the train journey, Sawat was so anxious that he asked a fellow passenger to look out for the po tree. The man reported that it was covered with white cloths. Sawat was staggered, and saw his elderly father jumping up and down, waving a piece of white cloth! The father hugged his son with tears of joy, and cried, 'I've been waiting for you.'

So God loves, forgives and waits for us.

'For this son of mine was dead and is alive again; he was lost and is found.'

Luke 15:24

---

1. Floyd McClung, *The Father Heart of God* (Eastbourne: Kingsway Publications, 1985).

4.
A gospel of love

IN June 2001 I visited Gartan, County Donegal, where St Columba was born of royal parents in AD 521. The Irish call him Colmcille, which means 'dove of the Church'. He was a missionary, statesman and poet, and is revered by all the major Christian denominations.

Columba attended various monastic schools, and in 546 founded his first monastery at Deny, followed by many others over the next seventeen years. Columba then led a battle against High King Diarmid in County Sligo, possibly concerning infringement of copyright; 3,000 warriors were killed. Columba was exiled, and sailed with twelve disciples to Southend, Kintyre, where his footprints are preserved on a rock; but he decided not to settle within sight of Ireland, so he sailed on via Dunadd to Iona ('island of my heart') where he spent the next thirty-four years, founding a monastery there and setting up over fifty ecclesiastical foundations on the mainland. He journeyed with two companions to see King Brude of the Picts at Inverness, who allowed him to preach his gospel of co-operation, neighbourliness and love throughout Pictland.

In 574, Columba chose and anointed Aidan as the first king of a united Scotland in Iona Abbey. He was seated on the Black Stone of Iona, which is now in the coronation chair at Westminster Abbey.

St Columba greatly admired St John the Baptist, and wore his flower (the yellow St John's Wort) inside his robe. He loved animals and birds, and set up a dispensary for them in Iona. He also loved children and gave women a more honourable place in society.

On 9 June 597 he died, kneeling beside the Abbey altar; the whole building shone with heavenly light reflected on his face.

> *… in all things God works for the good of those who love him …*
>
> **Romans 8:28**

5.
A neighbour in a million

IN Winchester in the flat opposite mine lived Dorothy. I was privileged to know her for the last five years of her life, until her death in January 2002, aged ninety-two.

No one could have been a better neighbour than Dorrie.

Whenever I got back from my frequent trips away there would always be a note with my post saying, 'Welcome back.' 'Well,' she would say, 'it's not much fun arriving home to an empty flat.' When Mother died, Dorrie told me to drop in if I felt lonely. She loved visits, being for some time housebound, and she always thanked me for coming in; but it was a pleasure.

Dorrie was very well read because she had not had the opportunity to travel much, so spent her spare time reading. Also, to keep mentally active, she did crosswords and watched *Countdown* on TV.

Dorrie enjoyed sharing her gifts of fruit and flowers. She was an accomplished seamstress and helped me with alterations.

When I took her some baking or did a fortnightly shop, she was most appreciative. Her sense of humour remained even when she was suffering physically. We liked watching *Keeping up Appearances* together on BBC 1.

Dorrie was a very spiritual person. She listened to *The Daily Service* at 9.45am on Radio 4 Longwave and watched the Sunday morning service (now sadly defunct) and *Songs of Praise* on BBC 1. Every week I took her a tape of my church's sermon. She would cut out my stories in the *NewsEXTRA*, and when in hospital found them of comfort.

After Dorrie died, her daughter gave me a large pile of her religious books. The most invaluable proved to be *A Concordance to the Holy Scriptures on the basis of Cruden* edited by Rev Professor John Eadie. This concordance helped me to check suitable Bible quotes for articles when my memory proved hazy. In the front of one of Dorrie's books she had written:

> **Trust in the LORD with all your heart …**
> **In all your ways acknowledge him,**
> **And he shall direct your paths.**
>
> **Proverbs 3:5–6**

6.
A symbol of hope in jail

WHEN Singapore fell to the Japanese in 1942, Ethel Mulvaney, a Canadian, was working there for the Red Cross.

Along with more than 4,000 internees, she was locked in Changi Jail, which had been built to accommodate just 400 prisoners. They suffered four years of crowding and hunger, flies and filth, with loneliness and isolation, and no news of family at home. Sometimes it seemed as though even God had forsaken them.

As the first Easter approached, this brave Red Cross worker went on behalf of the other women to ask the officer in charge of the prison if they might sing hymns in the courtyard on Easter morning. 'Why?' the officer asked. 'Because Christ rose from the dead on Easter morning,' Ethel replied. 'No,' he barked. 'Return to the compound.'

Twelve times this strange little drama of request and refusal was repeated. Then, to their astonishment came the order: 'Women prisoners may sing for five minutes in courtyard number 1, Changi Jail, at dawn on Easter morning.' In the presence of one guard they sang for five minutes, in which they praised God for Christ's resurrection, the only hope to which they could cling.

Silently they marched back, and as Mrs Mulvaney entered the passageway, the guard stepped up, reached under his brown shirt and drew out a tiny orchid. Placing it in her hand he said very softly: 'Yes, Christ did rise. I know it's true just as you do.' And with that he turned and was gone.

Mrs Mulvaney stood there, her eyes brimming with tears, knowing that she and the others need never again feel completely forsaken in Changi Jail. Someone else shared with them the Easter faith.

About midnight Paul and Silas were praying and singing hymns to God, and the other prisoners were listening to them.

Acts 16:25

7.
Amazing birds

OUR beautiful swallow, with its long-streamered tail and steel-blue, chestnut and white plumage, winters in South Africa but makes the tremendously long journey of 6,000 miles to the UK to breed – often using the same nest it has occupied for many years.

Swallows begin to arrive in ones or twos at the end of March – hence the age-old saying 'One swallow does not make a summer'. The majority come in mid or late April and leave in the autumn, when they can be seen gathering with their young on telephone wires.

Not until the nineteenth century did European explorers begin to discover the miracle of swallows' migration, increasingly confirmed by scientific ringing which in England began in 1909. The bird weighs about the same as a pound coin, measures seven and a half inches and lives on flying insects. However, when a swallow crosses the Sahara Desert, it has to survive 700 miles with little food or water, or fly hundreds of miles further by circumventing the desert. When traversing the Mediterranean Sea, it may get shot by hunters, although this is illegal. The English Channel presents the last major challenge because of changeable weather.

The migrants build nests of damp mud and grasses lined with feathers, on ledges and rafters – often in farm outbuildings. Females lay four to five eggs, which hatch in a fortnight; the nestlings can fly in three weeks. Two, sometimes three, broods are raised.

Like the swallow, we are all on a journey. For some of us it is harder than for others, but we will not discover true peace until we find our journey's end in God, the Father of us all.

Even the sparrow has found a home, and the swallow a nest for herself, where she may have her young – a place near your altar, O Lord Almighty, my King and my God.

Psalm 84:3

8.
God's providence

IT is always heartening when good news follows bad, as happened to me in Majorca some years ago.

Our plane back to Gatwick was delayed for four hours, which meant a total wait of six hours, from 4–10pm.

I was in a party of sixteen, one of whom suggested he and I should sit where other tourists were sitting watching the runway.

About 7.30pm, we were both feeling hungry and Bob said he would go and get himself some sandwiches. I agreed to save his seat for him and get something to eat when he returned.

The lady opposite gave me a drink from her giant bottle of orangeade. Then an English lady appeared and asked me if my plane was delayed. I answered, 'Yes.'

She did not inquire which airline, nor for how long, but simply handed me a box of delicious food while I uttered an amazed 'Thank you!' No one else in our party received such a thing, which had the emblem of a hotel on its side.

Bob then returned with his sandwiches and could not believe my good luck. He only got a few biscuits from the box (as did the lady with the orangeade) because I wanted to keep the surplus for breakfast at Gatwick!

On the train home at 8am the following day, a young lady asked the ticket collector if there was a buffet car. 'No,' came the reply. 'It's Sunday.' So I gave her one of my rolls, butter and jam.

When I told a church friend of my experience, he said the donor of the box was an angel, and this was God's provision for one of His children.

Men ate the bread of angels ...

Psalm 78:25

9.
Be persistent in your prayers

IN May 2003, the Women's Tuesday Afternoon
Fellowship of the Winchester Baptist Church held
its ninety-fourth anniversary service. The speaker was
the Reverend Kathryn Morgan from Portsmouth.
The congregation consisted of women from thirty
different churches. The Reverend Morgan spoke of
the importance of women in the Bible. There was
the Virgin Mary, whose prayer, the Magnificat, occurs
after the Annunciation by the Angel Gabriel that she
will bear a child called Jesus. Thirty years later, at the
wedding in Cana, she tells the stewards to listen to Jesus
and obey Him. He then turns the water into wine. At
His crucifixion, she is standing watching with John the
disciple when Jesus asks them to take care of each other.

After Jesus' resurrection, it is to Mary Magdalene that
He first appears, and tells her to take the good news to
the disciples; but they do not believe it.

When Paul, Luke and Silas were at Troas, Paul had a
vision of a man calling him to Macedonia, so they set off
and eventually reached Philippi. Outside this important
city was Lydia, a dealer in purple cloth, who loved God

and wanted to learn more about Him. She was in a women's fellowship, praying near some water. Paul baptised them all. He called women 'fellow workers', and many people greeted in his epistles were female.

Kathryn Morgan concluded, 'I come across many who pray, especially for the community and our world. Be persistent in prayer; it is the powerhouse to begin and sustain any work for God.'

I myself have been amazingly blessed by prayer. The rent of my flat was escalating, and I did not have sufficient income to meet it. Not a single estate agent in Winchester could help, nor the council. So I asked my friends and family to pray. Only one housing association had anything suitable, but I had to test if it was God's will. It took twenty minutes to walk to church from my existing flat and twenty minutes from the proposed new one! Inside the church door was a list of house groups – and there was one right nearby. I displayed a notice there of all the items I needed. Everything was supplied: either by church members, friends or relatives; and, incredibly, everything matched.

Do not be anxious about anything, but in everything, by prayer and petition, with thanksgiving, present your requests to God.

Philippians 4:6

10.
Honouring God

IN the corner of my new sitting room I hung a picture which came from my late father's study, depicting Christ's head crowned with thorns. Upon asking two Christians if this was a good place for it, they replied, 'No; it would be better in your bedroom.'

I followed their advice. However, some time after their deaths, while I was listening to *Sunday Half Hour* on Radio 2, during Charles Wesley's hymn 'O Thou who camest from above', Jesus rebuked me, saying, 'Put *Me* in the centre of your sitting room wall, so that I am seen first by any visitors; and as a reminder to you in your daily Quiet Time, as you sit opposite, that I suffered for your sins and must be Lord of your home.'

After two students had been to lunch, one of them wrote: 'We felt the presence of Jesus as soon as we entered your flat.'

As a constant reminder of God's rescuing love is a meaningful picture called 'The Lost Sheep': it hangs in my bathroom. I first saw it in the small Chapel of Christ's Suffering at Crowhurst Christian Healing Centre, East Sussex. The unknown artist depicts Jesus as the Good Shepherd, perilously reaching down over a steep cliff to save a fallen sheep. Hovering above the valley below is a vulture, symbolising Satan waiting to devour the errant creature. Christ is clearly risking His life, to protect us from evil and death.

Selwyn Hughes laboured towards the revival of Christianity throughout the world. Thus inspired, I now sing during my daily Quiet Time: 'Restore, O Lord,/The honour of Your name,/In works of sovereign power/Come shake the earth again. That men may see/And come with reverent fear/To the living God/Whose kingdom shall outlast the years'.[1]

'Those who honour me I will honour …'

1 Samuel 2:30

1. Extract taken from the song 'Restore, O Lord' by Graham Kendrick & Chris Rolinson. Copyright © 1981 Thankyou Music. Used by permission.*
This article, written in December 2010, did not appear in the *NewsEXTRA*.

11.
David beats adversity

WHILE on holiday at Southbourne, Bournemouth one September, I met a disabled man who greatly inspired me.

David and I fell into conversation during an hour's journey on an open-top bus.

David had wanted to teach, but then decided to work in the Oxford Travel Centre for British Rail, and later for their Sealink ferries at Weymouth. A friend got him a voluntary job at the royal estate of Balmoral before he had further employment in Bournemouth Travel Centre and notched up a total of twenty-nine years with British Rail.

David became a Christian when aged forty, at St John's Church, Weymouth. When I met him he was living with his parents in Southbourne, and was a member of Elim Pentecostal Church, Springbourne.

In 1996, aged forty-six, David got meningitis and was in hospital in a coma for two weeks. 'A nurse thought I was dying, but I revived. I was given physiotherapy, but it was too late to stop the death of muscles and nerves in my left foot. Now I have to wear a plastic splint and use a walking stick.'

David is not at all bitter about his situation and is a delight to converse with. He said, 'I'm fifty-three but I feel like thirty-three. Three days a week I attend a day centre, referred by Social Services. Apart from trying to play table tennis and learning to swim for the first time, I'm helping seven stroke victims to read and write again. I never give up hope on anyone.'

St Paul said:

And now these three remain: faith, hope and love. But the greatest of these is love.

1 Corinthians 13:13

Beech wood

The way through the wood is narrow,
Tree trunks close me in
On either side, like an avenue,
A gigantic cathedral so high
I can scarcely see the canopy
Of beech leaves against the sky.

When people crowd around me
And drain my strength away,
I go to the wood to recuperate
And hear what God has to say.

It's a steep climb to the top of a tree,
There is no branch to hold on to,
Just faith that eventually I'll see
God's beauty in all its fullness,
His gift to you and to me.

I cannot perceive a turning
At the end of the path I tread,
However much I long to know
The road that lies ahead.
I just must keep on walking,
Trusting God for every step,
Until I reach the Promised Land
Where He will hold me in His hand.

12.
Do not grieve – give thanks

MY father had accepted an invitation to preach at his old school on Remembrance Sunday. He was seventy-two years old and used to caring for elderly people at a church in Bournemouth. The script was sent to me, but I knew it would not appeal to the wriggling small boys or the cynical teenagers. So I sent back suggestions for a substantial re-write. Mother was annoyed; but I was putting the boys first.

I prayed fervently as Father got up to speak. He said afterwards that he could feel me rooting for him! Best of all, the small boys were listening avidly as he told wartime tales of Goodmayes, Essex, where he earned the nickname Mr Mop because he was always helping people sweep up following a bombing.

After the service we went down to the playing fields, where he showed me the rugger posts over which he had scored a very high try. 'A reporter from Wellington filed a story about it in his paper. When I die I don't want you to grieve. Just give thanks I had such a wonderful sporting life here. And sprinkle my ashes on the cricket pitch.'

It was one of the hardest things I have had to do.

Mother spent her last year in a care home. She was eighty-six, and suffered from Alzheimer's disease. As death approached, I prayed aloud for forgiveness for the times we had hurt each other. Her last words were: 'Look after Roderick [my Dad], when I'm gone.' So I reminded her, 'Roderick is in heaven waiting for you!' – at which she gave a little laugh of joy.

Mother wanted her ashes sprinkled in Mortehoe cemetery, North Devon, because Morte Point was where as a family we had many happy walks. However, the undertaker said it would be very difficult to get permission, so I decided to scatter the ashes on the rocks of the Point. For music, a stonechat sang cheerfully, and sea pinks paid a floral tribute. We had had a beautiful cremation and church service nine months earlier, but this final laying to rest was nonetheless moving in its simplicity. So all was well that ended well.

'… we look forward eagerly to the day when we shall have heavenly bodies which we shall put on like new clothes. For we shall not be merely spirits without bodies.'
2 Corinthians 5:2–3 (TLB)

13.
Don't despair of errant children

SEPTEMBER 1982 marked the 300th anniversary of the founding of Pennsylvania, USA and its capital, Philadelphia, by the Quaker William Penn.

Yet Penn's rise to fame was not unmarred by rows with his wealthy father, similar to many a parent–teenage conflict today. Then, as now, having the courage to speak one's mind always brought trouble – trouble which had to be surmounted boldly in order that justice might prevail. For his strongly held, nonconformist beliefs, Penn was expelled from Christ Church, Oxford, and received a thrashing from his father – the redoubtable Admiral whose armour hangs on the north wall of the nave of St Mary Redcliffe Church, Bristol. And on his return from adequately administering his father's Irish estate he was turned out of doors because his conscience prevented him from raising his hat to anyone – great or lowly. Yet it was the Duke of York who helped get him out of the Tower of London, where he was imprisoned for publishing *The Sandy Foundation Shaken*.

One might expect a man of William Penn's determined character and achievements to have been proud and unforgiving. On the contrary, his own gravestone at Jordans Friends' Meeting House in Buckinghamshire is in the simple Quaker tradition, bearing just his name and dates of birth and death on a plain slab. But for his father he composed an impressive epitaph of his accomplishments, displayed on an elaborate memorial at St Mary Redcliffe, Bristol. Furthermore, he wrote such an inspired conception of the transience of death that a modern-day curate, the Reverend Peter Clark, used it at every funeral service he conducted.

Does one need further proof that anxious parents need never totally despair of their seemingly errant offspring – provided they remain true to their own convictions?

'… your word is truth.'
John 17:17

14.
Don't forget to say thank you

A SMALL boy was eager to leave the railway station on his way home from boarding school for the Christmas holidays.

'Have you thanked the driver?' asked his father.

'No, Dad.'

'Then back you go, right to the end of the platform. Don't you realise you owe your life to that man?'

When the boy grew up, he never forgot to say 'thank you'. Once, on returning from holiday in Guernsey, he disappeared at the airport. Then his wife spotted him far out on the runway. She smiled in relief. 'He's gone to thank the pilot for a safe flight!'

The adage 'Praise where you can, blame where you must' certainly works. If we have valid complaints against powerful organisations, they can be surprisingly helpful if we first acknowledge something they do which is worthwhile.

Giving thanks to God can be a very positive way to start each day. And the Arab saying 'I felt sad because I had no shoes – until I saw a man with no feet' bears thinking about when we visit those tempting stores. And if we can't afford to buy gifts, it doesn't matter. Let's remember to give thanks for the things that really count – like friendship.

My happiest Christmas occurred when I had nothing to put into the church collection except a book of stamps. For the first time in forty years I understood God's greatest gift. He sent Jesus as a helpless infant into the poverty of this world.

Let's remember to give thanks at Christmas for the wealth that is ours in Jesus.

One of them, when he saw he was healed, came back, praising God in a loud voice. He threw himself at Jesus' feet and thanked him …

Luke 17:15–16

15.
Enough to melt the hardest of hearts

THE village of Igls in Austria really woke up for Christmas. Advent wreaths of spruce and silver bells hung from door knockers and in the shops one heard a babel of English, American drawl, French, Hochdeutsch and Austrian dialect as people scrambled to buy lebkuchen (iced gingerbread biscuits), Christmas cake (sultana and raisin bread dusted with icing sugar) and posies of chocolate flowers.

Each day, more cars arrived, fitted with roof racks to carry skis. The visitors provided a colourful fashion parade in ski wear against the dazzling white snow.

From across the square came the ethereal melody of *Stille Nacht* – first performed at Oberndorf near Salzburg in 1818. The choir stood around an illumined Christmas tree, while the steeple of the yellow stuccoed church pointed to a star-spangled sky.

Among elaborate wreaths beside the gravestones flickered slow burning candles: red, white and gold. A crowd of holidaymakers had gathered, and when the last carol ended there was a murmur of expectation.

All the children of Igls were about to present their Christmas Eve pageant.

First came Joseph guiding a tiny donkey pulling a rough cart on which sat Mary, holding a live baby in the folds of her blue cloak. Shepherds followed: young boys in skins and hairy cloaks, leading sheep; older lads carried bleating lambs on their shoulders. Others solemnly held lanterns and crooks. A group of pilgrims in old Austrian costume walked closely on their heels, aided by alpenstocks. Finally, the angelic host appeared, clothed in white with wings and silver haloes, each face radiant in the candlelight they carried.

The noisiest members of the crowd stood silent; the hardest hearts were melted.

Jesus said, 'Let the little children come to me, and do not hinder them, for the kingdom of heaven belongs to such as these.'

Matthew 19:14

16.
Everyone is entitled to at least one day of rest

WHEN I was living with my parents, my father would not allow me to play any sport on a Sunday which would result in others having to work. And Great Aunt Belle told me that as a child she was not permitted to sew on Sundays because every stitch was a stitch in the side of Jesus. In my opinion, both were rather extreme views.

The Pharisees attacked Jesus on the Sabbath for letting His hungry disciples pluck ears of corn, and for healing the sick. Jesus replied, 'It is lawful to do good on the Sabbath' (Matthew 12:12).

The reason for the Pharisees' anger was that, in the old story of the world's creation, God rested on the seventh day. When Moses received the Ten Commandments, one of them was 'Remember the Sabbath day to keep it holy'.

Everyone needs at least one day off per week to recuperate from work and routine chores. I try not to wash clothes, do ironing, cleaning or shopping on a Sunday. For me, it is a chance to go to church to worship God, to listen to His voice, to find spiritual uplift from hymns and sermon, and to meet the many friends I've made in various Christian denominations.

It saddened me when as a nation we chose to make Sunday like any other day, which enabled employers to put pressure on their employees to work on a Sunday, with adverse effect on church going and family life. Jesus always went to the synagogue on the Sabbath, and the Queen attends church every Sunday, no matter where in the world she is.

Many Christians backed the Keep Sunday Special Campaign, but the majority won; that is democracy. However, sometimes the few are wiser than the many.

Then he said to them, 'The Sabbath was made for man, not man for the Sabbath.'

Mark 2:27

17.
Find some time to think

TRAVELLING by train to Bristol some years ago, I met a charming lady called Jenny Streeter from Lindfield, West Sussex. I had just bought a copy of *Unexpected Healing* by Jennifer Rees Larcombe. When Jenny saw it she exclaimed, 'I know that lady – she comes from Tunbridge Wells and was eight years in a wheelchair until healed by God.'

Jenny Streeter belonged to an evangelical Anglican church with twenty-four house groups. Her own group was studying *Open Home, Open Bible* [1] with a video by Richard Bewes, then Rector of All Souls, Langham Place in London. I myself had visited this lively church some years ago.

Michael, Jenny's husband, was asked to retire early, and since then had served the Lord in many different ways, such as being administrator for a scheme based in the Diocese of Chichester called Growing Healthy Churches, which is of great help to church leaders.

Their daughter was in Bulgaria, where she had set up a foundation supporting the disabled in their homes. By coincidence, the Streeters knew a family in Winchester, supported at that time by my church.

In 1968, when Michael and Jenny were waiting to move into a new home, a Baptist lady put them up in her attic room. Her adage was, 'Look back with gratitude, look forward with hope, look up with confidence.'

Towards the end of our journey we discussed the biblical story of Martha, Mary and their brother Lazarus, who were good friends of Jesus. Jenny thought Martha was over the top in busyness compared with her contemplative sister Mary. We often find ourselves too busy because of today's hectic lifestyle. Jesus calls us to stop and spend time with Him.

'Be still, and know that I am God ...'

Psalm 46:10

---

1. Richard Bewes, *Open Home, Open Bible* (London: Hodder & Stoughton, 1991).

18.
Forgiveness

CORRIE ten Boom and her sister Betsie were imprisoned by the Nazis for harbouring Jews in their Dutch home during the Second World War. They were keen Christians and their faith kept them alive in the most terrible conditions at Vught, and then at the notorious Ravensbruck concentration camp.

They managed to hide their Bible and read from it twice a day to their fellow prisoners. Theology and denominationalism were irrelevant when they all faced death every day. Corrie would ask them individually: 'Do you know that Jesus died for the sins of the whole world, also for your sins, and that He loves you? Did you give your heart to Him? Did you confess your sins to Him and repent?' If the answer was 'Yes', Corrie knew the prisoner was safe in the care of Jesus, no matter what happened.

Betsie saw good in almost everything, thanking God for the fleas in the barracks because they kept the guards away, and praying for the guards as for the prisoners. She had a vision of a lovely home set in a garden – a retreat for disturbed refugees. Betsie died four days before Corrie was released, and Corrie immediately set about discovering such a house, eventually finding it in Bloemendaal. Through the years she visited sixty-four countries and spoke before millions of people, telling prison stories and of the love of God and the refugee home.

Corrie was asked to visit a prison where a former Nazi guard, Carl, was interned. She had known him at Vught. He held out his hand, saying: 'Fraulein, I too have become a Christian.' After great inner struggle, Corrie shook hands with him. She remembered that Jesus told us to love our enemies and that He helps us to be channels of His love. After her visit she requested a reprieve for Carl from Queen Juliana because he had accepted Jesus as Saviour.

'Love your enemies and pray for those who persecute you …'
Matthew 5:44

Forgiveness

O the blessedness of forgiveness,
When we can let go the sins of others
That hurt us to the very core of our being
And stunt us in our Christian growth.

Yet, if we hold on to the pain,
We will only reap bitterness,
And this will damage our very souls.
So we must ask Christ to enter each situation
And feel our sufferings as if His own.

Then we can forgive our transgressors
And lift them to Him on the cross
So He can heal us and restore our spirits.

Two aconites

A grim time we had of it,
Struggling … you and I,
Up through the dark dank earth
Until we could see the sky.

We thought we'd never make it –
The journey seemed so long:
Roots of trees were treacherous –
Winter harsh and strong.

But one by one, in searching,
We broke the heavy clod.
And now we shine like gold drops
Reflecting the Son of God!

19.
Fulfilling the words of the prophet Zechariah

SEVERAL times Jesus had warned His disciples to expect opposition and suffering at the hands of the authorities in Jerusalem. He had even spoken of betrayal, mocking, flogging and crucifixion. Nevertheless, their spirits rose, for they were going with Jesus to share the Passover Feast, the greatest festival of the Jewish year.

Two miles outside the city, two disciples approached, leading a donkey colt with its mother. They threw their cloaks over the colt and Jesus sat on it. He was deliberately fulfilling the ancient words of the prophet Zechariah: 'See, your king comes to you, righteous and having salvation, gentle and riding on a donkey …' (Zechariah 9:9). Jesus was coming in peace. The crowds shouted 'Blessed is he who comes in the name of the Lord!' (Matthew 21:9), threw down their cloaks before Jesus and waved palm branches.

But Jesus posed a threat to the authorities – both Jewish and Roman. He headed towards the Temple and began to overthrow the tables of the money changers and the dove sellers, who had become a symbol of corruption.

'And he said to them, "It is written, My house shall be called a house of prayer," but you have made it a 'den of thieves'"' (Matthew 21:13, NKJV). The blind and the lame came to Him at the Temple and He healed them. Excluded for centuries, now they were being welcomed in.

Jesus returned as God's Son to God's Holy City as King over earthly powers and as Lord over the Temple, while His healing work symbolises His true mission. Jesus afflicts the comfortable and comforts the afflicted.

When Jesus entered Jerusalem, the whole city was stirred ... 'This is Jesus, the prophet from Nazareth in Galilee.'
Matthew 21:10–11

The above account was taken, with permission, from the Reverend Jonathan Scamman's sermon preached at Christ Church, Winchester in March 2004.

20.
Gift saved baby's life

DR HELEN Roseveare, a missionary doctor in what is now the Democratic Republic of Congo, relates in her book *Living Faith*,[1] the wonderful story of God's answer to a child's prayer.

One night, Helen had struggled in vain to save the life of a woman in labour, who left behind a premature baby and a crying two-year-old daughter. There was no electricity for an incubator and, despite living on the equator, nights could be cold. A student midwife collected a box and cotton wool in which to wrap the baby. Another stoked up the fire and went to fetch a hot water bottle. The bottle burst; it was the last one.

The following noon, as usual, Helen held a voluntary prayer meeting with the orphanage children. Ruth, aged ten, prayed: 'Please God, send us a water bottle. It will be no good tomorrow, God, as the baby will be dead, so please send it this afternoon. And while you are about it, would You please send a dolly for the little girl so she'll know You really love her.'

When Helen went home that afternoon, there was a parcel on the veranda weighing twenty-two pounds.

She sent for the thirty to forty orphanage children, who gazed as she pulled out various gifts, including a new hot water bottle. Ruth cried out: 'If God has sent the hot water bottle, He must have sent the dolly too!' She proceeded to find it at the bottom of the box.

The parcel had taken five months to reach Helen. It had been packed by her former Sunday school class, whose leader had obeyed God's prompting to send a hot water bottle, even to the equator. One of the girls had put in a dolly for an African child.

'Before they call I will answer …'

Isaiah 65:24

1. Dr Helen Roseveare, *Living Faith* (Grand Rapids: Bethany House Publishers, 1980).

21.
Giving children a hand to help themselves

'SOME children have no clothes to come to school. It would make them happy if they had some,' was a child's comment at a children's club in Tajikistan, near Afghanistan.

Some years ago I attended a Save the Children seminar in Winchester called Beat Poverty. Founded in 1919, Save the Children is the world's largest independent children's charity. It is now a US$1.3 billion global organisation, working in 117 countries facing environmental problems and poverty.[1] The United Nations defines absolute poverty as having 70p or less to live on per day.

Sylvie Baird, a corporate fundraising executive, told the story of seventeen-year-old Mirzovali from a village about 100 kilometres from Dushanbe, capital of Tajikistan. He and his mother and two sisters fled to Dushanbe during the civil war of 1992–1997. His mother now worked in the market, while Mirzovali washed cars to help support one sister through her studies. He attended a drop-in centre run by a partner of Save the

Children, which helped young people to secure jobs. They could learn sewing, English, electrical repairs and traditional drumming, which enabled them to play at weddings and birthday parties.

'If ever I get rich, I would like to open another huge centre, with food provided for street children, so they could receive more education,' Mirzovali said. When Sylvie told him how people in the UK support Save the Children, he replied: 'God will bless them,' (a Muslim expression of thanks).

Jesus said:

'And whoever welcomes a little child like this in my name welcomes me. But if anyone causes one of these little ones who believe in me to sin, it would be better for him to have a large millstone hung around his neck and to be drowned in the depths of the sea.'

Matthew 18:5–6

---

1. Source: www.savethechildren.net (accessed 3 November 2010).

22.
God calls all kinds of people

I **AM** indebted to Mike Carson – a lay reader at Christ
Church, Winchester – for his portrayal of one of my
favourite Bible stories.

Paul and Silas are beaten by the magistrates in Philippi
(Macedonia) for disturbing the city with their teaching;
and for silencing a slave girl with a demonic spirit who
tells fortunes. The apostles are thrown into jail; manacled
to stocks, yet sing hymns and say prayers at midnight.

There is an earthquake, and all doors and chains burst
open; the jailer fears the prisoners have escaped and
is about to kill himself. But Paul keeps them all there
and the jailer believes Paul is a god and wants to know
how he can be saved. In the middle of the night, the
jailer washes the two men's wounds; then he and all his
household are baptised and he gives the two disciples a
meal in his house.

As Paul and Silas are Roman citizens they refuse to
leave until the magistrates come in person to release
them, for a Roman citizen had special rights. They then
go to Lydia's home and enjoy hospitality.

The Jews' daily prayer was to thank God that they were

not Gentiles, women or slaves, but the slave girl, the jailer and Lydia show that God calls all sorts of people.

The story of Christ on the cross has some parallels with that of Paul and Silas. Christ had an unfair trial, Paul and Silas had none. Both Pilate and magistrates ordered severe floggings. Earthquakes occurred in each event, breaking the power of sin and death, setting people free.

They [Paul and Silas] replied: 'Believe in the Lord Jesus, and you will be saved – you and your household.'

Acts 16:31

23.
Sense of belonging

GRAM Seed was a ne'er-do-well. He grew up in Middlesbrough and fought with everyone. When aged about twelve, he broke into schools and youth clubs, selling all he could steal.

At fifteen, charged with twenty-two offences of burglary, the court sentenced him to nine months in a juvenile institution. After that, he was often in prison. Working in the middle of organised crime, he amassed wealth from dealing in counterfeit goods. Yet for three years until 1996 he lived on a street bench taking drugs and trying to drink himself to death.

Later that year, Gram collapsed in his council flat and was taken to hospital. The doctors found he had pneumonia, hypothermia, severe malnutrition, severe dehydration and liver and kidney failure. Even after several days' treatment they could not rouse him from his coma. But his mother begged them not to give up.

Then came a group of Christian lads Gram knew on the streets. They laid hands on him and said: 'In the name of Jesus Christ of Nazareth, give this man life.' Gram came round and recovered.

Gram found a room with a friend, but the Christian lads still visited. They persuaded him to join an Alpha course at their church because he asked so many questions about Jesus. He received the Holy Spirit with a surge of love in his heart. 'All my life I'd never belonged to anyone. I was a misfit, and here I was belonging to someone at last.'

Gram is now married with two sons. He visits prisons regularly to help with Alpha courses and to tell prisoners about Jesus Christ.

Since 2008, CWR has published two autobiographical books by Gram: *One Step Beyond* and *It Must Be Love*, together with a DVD. He has also established Sowing Seeds Ministries, a Christian charity which brings the message of the love of Christ to young prisoners and ex offenders. Thanks to the wonderful response to CWR's appeal to raise funds to donate copies of Gram's first book to prisoners currently serving sentences, 20,000 were sent into UK prisons via chaplains.

In October 2001, Gram gave me permission to relate his experiences and wrote: 'I hope and pray my story can be used to glorify Jesus everywhere. God bless.'

For God so loved the world that he gave his one and only Son, that whoever believes in him shall not perish but have eternal life.

John 3:16

24.
Goodness behind a nightmare past

'WHEN we read the gospels, we meet a different Jesus from the one we see in the stained glass windows of churches where you must not laugh or make a noise. Maybe that is why you do not often see joyful people running to church to pray,' writes David Rhodes in *Lenten Adventure*.[1]

Jesus often consorted with those whom the scribes and Pharisees branded as unclean, and the most saintly men in the Gospels smelt of fish, sweat and wine.

St Luke tells of a street woman who entered the house of Simon the Pharisee where Jesus was dining (Luke 7:36–50). She washed His dusty feet with her tears, dried them with her hair, kissed them ceaselessly and anointed them with ointment. Simon rebuked Jesus for allowing such a woman to minister to Him, but the Lord said that her many sins had been forgiven because she had loved much.

Mary Magdalene was a prostitute with seven demons, and these had to be exorcised by Jesus before she could reform her life and follow Him. She was the first to see Him resurrected on Easter morning and was told to carry the good news to the disciples.

David Rhodes gave spiritual direction for some years to a prostitute called Eve, who had suffered child abuse. But after the first twenty minutes, he found that Eve taught him more about God than anyone else he had ever met: 'Each time we met, I felt I was being touched by the Kingdom of God. And each time we talk on the phone the same thing happens. Somewhere in her damaged and nightmarish past something very strange happened to Eve. Instead of becoming more defensive and hiding herself away behind a protective mask, she has become even more open and honest.'[2]

> *... Jesus said, 'It is not the healthy who need a doctor, but the sick ... For I have not come to call the righteous, but sinners.'*
>
> **Matthew 9:12–13**

---

1. David Rhodes, *Lenten Adventure* (London: SPCK Publishing, 2000).
2. Ibid.

Treasured tears

A pearl drop hung upon my brow:
Luminous, opaque and lustrous.
No other jewels were needed,
For, as the intellect was laid aside,
I found the pearl of great price
Buried deep within my heart.

Without shame I claim
His cross –
His mark upon my brow,
His thorns, His tears
That turn to pearls,
Pearls without price.

25.
Healing rifts worldwide

THE Corrymeela Community was set up in 1965 by the inspiration of the Reverend Ray Davey, a prisoner-of-war chaplain in Nazi Germany. The community is committed to this statement of faith: 'A people of all ages and Christian traditions who individually and together are committed to the healing of social, religious and political divisions that exist in Northern Ireland and throughout the world.'

Each year more than 7,000 people visit the Corrymeela Centre, whose name means 'Hill of Harmony'. The residential centre is at Ballycastle cliff top, on the North Antrim coast of Northern Ireland. In addition, the community currently has over 150 members, largely lay people, who live out their commitment to peace and reconciliation in their homes, workplaces, churches and local communities in the Province.

An amazing mixture of people from different communities in forty different countries visit the Corrymeela international summer school. It is a place of respite and safety. The community also runs activities and programmes bringing groups together from all educational backgrounds to discuss politics, religion and the culture of different traditions. There are groups for women, single parents and bereaved families. Support is also given to Residents' Associations, many from places which have been badly affected by conflict.

There are a number of Corrymeela support groups throughout Britain. Every year, Corrymeela invites churches to hold a Sunday service to explore an aspect of reconciliation. In March 2003, I attended such a service at the United Church, Winchester, on the theme 'Conflict and Community'. Corrymeela's experience in Northern Ireland has shown that reconciliation *is* possible.

Jesus said:

> *'A new command I give you: Love one another. As I have loved you, so you must love one another.'*
>
> **John 13:34**

26.
An influential man

SAUL of Tarsus, later known as Paul, was a very strict Jew and a tentmaker by occupation. The chief persecutor of the early followers of Jesus, he became the first and greatest missionary. Because of him, a small sect grew into a worldwide faith.

In AD 36, three years after Jesus' crucifixion and resurrection, Saul was on the way to Damascus to arrest Jewish converts to Christianity. He was struck down and blinded for three days by a brilliant light. A voice said, 'I am Jesus, whom you are persecuting … Now get up and go into the city, and you will be told what you must do' (Acts 9:5–6).

Saul was baptised in Damascus, and subsequently told the Jews to accept Gentiles (non-Jews) as believers without inflicting Jewish laws on them.

Paul went to Philippi in AD 50 and baptised Lydia, the first convert in Europe. In the city of Corinth, he preached against the citizens' immoral behaviour. He had to escape from Ephesus for condemning the worship of the goddess Artemis, which brought in huge incomes.

In AD 58, Paul brought Gentile money to Jerusalem

for the church. Rioters tried to kill him, and he was sent to the Roman governor in Caesarea. He was imprisoned for two years and appealed to Caesar because he held Roman citizenship. Consequently, he travelled to Rome, where he was kept under house arrest for two years, although free to evangelise. Between AD 64–68, Paul was executed by Emperor Nero.

No other apostle suffered more imprisonments, floggings, shipwrecks or difficult journeys than St Paul, and a large number of his inspiring thirteen letters in the Bible were written in captivity.

I have fought the good fight, I have finished the race, I have kept the faith.

2 Timothy 4:7

27.
Into the unknown

AT some time in our lives, each of us has to walk into the unknown. If we were psychic and foresaw the pitfalls, we would stop and stagnate from indecision.

But the world's momentum demands that we move with it. This may entail finding or losing a job, a home, marriage, children, or perhaps suffering illness and ultimately death.

To walk through a dark tunnel requires faith. The light behind you recedes, the way ahead is uncertain. It must be a terrifying experience for young miners going underground for the first time, but they know others have been there before them. If, however, you are potholing or in search of an exciting cavern, you either trust a guide or you must venture on in blind faith.

What really counts is whether at the end of our own personal tunnel we reach enlightenment. This may not necessarily mean worldly success, wealth or popularity. On the contrary, it may involve shedding these very things because they are causing us to stumble. It may mean clearing the path from the rubble of our past.

Some of us need to slow down, to gain strength for

the journey, lest we arrive too breathless to enjoy the view at the end of the road. Others who dally over trivia perhaps ought to recall the words in Brahms' Requiem: 'Lord, teach me that I must come to an end, and my life has a goal.'

At Iona Abbey, on the fifteenth-century stone wall of the Founder's Room, is a poster which reads: 'Visionary people are visionary because of what they don't see.'

The Rev Dr George MacLeod had the vision in 1938 to rebuild the Abbey as a community of peace and Christian brotherhood open to all denominations. His unswerving faith brought him triumphantly through the tunnel of the unknown and made him a worthy successor to Scotland's greatest evangelist, St Columba.

For we walk by faith, not by sight.
2 Corinthians 5:7 (NKJV)

28.
Isaiah makes Mother's day

MY mother and I had been invited to the sixtieth birthday party of our cousin, a vicar in Poole. Mother, then aged eighty-four, suffered badly from arthritis and had pain in her arm following a fall.

Then she cracked the upper plate of her teeth and, although it was temporarily mended, she was afraid of a disaster at the lunch. Nevertheless, the night before, she ironed her best dress ready for the party. The next morning, however, she appeared at the door of her bedroom and said, 'I'm not going. And the hardest thing will be to convince *you*!'

I gave her a cup of tea and she retired to her bed to do her hip exercises. Meanwhile, I studied my Bible-reading scheme. The passage for that day was Isaiah 40:29–31: 'He gives strength to the weary and increases the power of the weak. Even youths grow tired and weary, and young men stumble and fall; but those who hope in the LORD will renew their strength.' (Used in *Every Day with Jesus* by Selwyn Hughes.)

I could not wait to share this passage with Mother, although sometimes she did not agree with my religious views. Today, however, was different. At 9.45am I asked if she would like *The Daily Service* on Radio 4, which she usually did. 'No, thank you. I'm still thinking about what you read to me,' she said. Without a word she put on her best dress and finely chopped some bread and meat to take with her.

Mother was seated next to her favourite cousin of the same age. She even managed two desserts – her favourite strawberry pavlova! The vicar's father, aged ninety and almost blind, made an amusing speech about his son's sixty years. Brave indeed, but the bravest guest of all was undoubtedly my mother; with thanks to Isaiah.

… your strength must come from the Lord's mighty power within you.

Ephesians 6:10 (TLB)

29.
Kindness can kill …

ST Kilda in the Outer Hebrides has the largest colony of gannets in the world. Its cliffs are the highest in Britain, rising to 1,300 feet. The Bass Rock off the east coast of Scotland (which I visited with the Scottish Ornithological Club) is also famous for these birds. They pair for life and produce one chick a year.

Parent gannets stuff their young with fish for the first two months, by which time they exceed adult weight.

Then, for over a month, the juveniles are abandoned until starvation forces them to volplane down to the sea. What are their thoughts as they plunge from paradise lost? Bewilderment, fear, perhaps even hate. What is the unseen force that drives them on?

On the sea they swim without being able to feed for as long as three weeks, attempting to fly so that they can dive from heights of up to 100 feet – which will take them deep into a new world to catch fish.

Many never learn to fly, and their bodies are found on the autumnal tide line.

Those that succeed find everything of which they dreamt. When soaring upwards to paradise regained, how glad they must be for taking the risk! Their grey down of doubt has been transfigured into gleaming white pinions of hope in the sunlight, though still tipped with black so that the past is not forgotten. No wonder the gannet, or Solan goose, used to be considered a royal delicacy.

How often we find that the hardest beginnings produce the strongest characters! No one really lives unless they have jumped into the unknown. Satiety without starvation breeds inertia, and kindness can kill.

Train a child in the way he should go,
and when he is old he will not turn from it.

Proverbs 22:6

30.
Learning from chance meetings

WHEN travelling about by rail, bus or on foot, I often meet people with something to teach me.

At Waterloo station a number of years ago, I provided myself with an almond croissant and a cup of coffee, as well as carrying a mac, carrier bag and handbag. The young African girl at the ticket barrier asked for my ticket. I stooped to put the cup of coffee on the ground, but she stopped me. 'I'll hold it, the ground's dirty.' Unfortunately, she spilt coffee on her timetable.

'I'm so sorry,' I said, using my handkerchief to mop the booklet.

'It's not your fault,' she smiled.

'No, but you were doing me a kindness.'

'God bless you,' she said after I finally produced my train ticket.

'Are you a Christian?' I asked.

'Yes.'

'So am I.'

'A Roman Catholic,' she added.

'Evangelical Anglican,' I replied. (I've since joined several other denominations.)

'Well,' she beamed. 'We all worship the same God. First stop Winchester.'

It was Basingstoke; but we can't get things right every time!

Shortly after this I was on the pavement at the foot of Oram's Arbour in Winchester when I became aware of someone coming up behind me with an uneven gait. I stepped sideways and saw a middle-aged man with muscle spasm in one hand and one foot. He told me he'd had cerebral palsy since birth.

'I live at St Cross,' he said, 'and I walk to the bottom of St Paul's Hill and back again [a distance of 3.6 miles] every day so as not to seize up. I go slowly or I get tired. And I have an hour's rest here on a bench.'

My own minor problems paled into insignificance against this man's, *and* he kept smiling. How important it is to learn from chance encounters!

'Is it nothing to you, all you who pass by?'
Lamentations 1:12

31.
Help for the homeless

IN May 2003, several churches in or near Winchester teamed up with On the Move, a Christian organisation from Birmingham which runs free barbecues.

On the first day, I helped give out leaflets to the 750 people who were fed.

Some homeless and unemployed folk said they didn't believe in God or Jesus; others helped me pick up litter and even gave me a welcome can of lager!

One young man said: 'I don't believe in God, because I prayed to Him for a home and He did not answer.' I replied: 'But you've just told me that the Social Services are getting you a bedsit in two weeks.' He declared: 'That's Social Services, not God.'

I explained to him that God could work through Social Services. His friend responded that Christianity is rubbish, but the young man rebuked him for knocking someone with a faith. 'I'm doing Community Service for theft of food and drink because I was hungry and thirsty and had no money. God won't forgive me, and I shall go to hell.'

'No you won't,' I assured him. 'If you ask God to forgive you, "as far as the east is from the west, so far [does] he remove our transgressions from us"' (Psalm 103:12).

On the Move states three steps are necessary to become a Christian: believe in God and thank Him for sending Jesus to die for you; ask forgiveness for the wrong things you have done; ask Jesus to come into your heart, and give your life to Him.

Jesus said:

'Here I am! I stand at the door and knock. If anyone hears my voice and opens the door, I will come in and eat with him, and he with me.'

Revelation 3:20

The simple things

Someone to share the simple things of life,
That's all I ask.
Is it too much, Lord,
To wish to share
Five loaves, two fish?
Or wander with another vibrant soul
Down leafy lanes dancing with sunlight
Through the tiny window panes of beech
Hemmed in by secret banks of bluebell, spurge
And carefree windflower?
Or in the twilight dusk
To watch together swifts ceaselessly scything across the sky;
And count the hours with laughter till the dawn
Bears on its pillowed clouds the day.
To tend each garden plant with care,
Charting its progress year by year,
And learn afresh the songs of youth.
Is it too much, Lord,
To wish to be happy?

32.
Love lives on

IN his book *Beyond Death's Door*, the American doctor Maurice Rawlings relates how many of his patients who temporarily died through cardiac arrest had vivid experiences of heaven or hell. Many were converted to Christianity as a result. John Wesley was proud to be able to say of his followers, 'They died well.' And a retired Methodist minister admitted happily: 'I've had a wonderful life, and I'm ready to go when the time comes.'

He insisted on renaming funerals as 'thanksgiving services' and in his will left instructions that no mournful music should be played, nor mourning apparel be worn by the congregation.

But a middle-aged, ordained headmaster confessed he is nonplussed as to what comfort to offer parents whose child dies. Victorian tombstones are a harrowing reminder of how recently a high rate of infant mortality was the norm. Yet Ann (MacVicar) Grant of Laggan, Scotland, who outlived eleven of her twelve children, shows in her published volumes of letters a growing spiritual strength which is often hard to find today.

If a widow ceaselessly harks back to her husband's last illness, it's easy to sympathise: 'Well, it was a happy release, wasn't it?' For him, maybe. But how about for her? The removal of accustomed male 'ballast' can often rock a wife's boat considerably. One widow stated resignedly: 'Half my life went when my husband died.'

The best comfort I ever received on the loss of a dear friend and mentor was my mother's words: 'She wouldn't want you to grieve. She'd say: "Go on! Keep writing!"' Sometimes the bereaved create both cathartic and eternal masterpieces in memory of loved ones: the Taj Mahal, and the inspiring Requiems of church music, for instance.

There are many sources, both biblical and secular – eg the writings of Jung – which sustain belief in an afterlife. As William Penn wrote on the death of his father in 1670, 'They that love beyond the world cannot be separated by it. Death cannot kill that which never dies. Nor can spirits ever be divided, that love and live in the same divine principle, the root and record of their friendship. If absence be not death, neither is theirs. Death is but crossing the world as friends do the seas. They live in one another still ...'[1]

Even though I walk through the valley of the shadow of death, I will fear no evil, for you are with me ...

Psalm 23:4

---

1. William Penn, *Some Fruits of Solitude / More Fruits of Solitude* (BiblioBazaar, 2009).

33.
Make sure you keep your battery charged

IN *Lenten Adventure*[1], David Rhodes describes how a lay assistant and retired builder called Big John was driving through a South African township when he gave a lift to a woman carrying a car battery. She was heading to a garage a mile away and would have to pay three rand to get the battery recharged. The battery powered the only source of light in the shack where she and her family lived.

Big John said he would recharge anyone's batteries for one and a half rand. He then helped them build a church and led its worship. Seventy-nine baptisms took place, and soon the church had to be extended.

On Christmas Eve 1984, when staying at a remote convent in Somerset, I walked for over half an hour in pitch darkness to reach a village church. Above me were hundreds of stars, and I recalled God's promise to Abraham that he would have that amount of descendants. Being unmarried and childless, this could only mean in my case *spiritual* children – followers of Jesus through my writings. When I got back to the convent I wrote a poem which I read to the nuns after my final lunch with them. Then I spoke a parable which God had given me while strolling in the country lanes:

'When you are a new Christian, you are so excited by your faith that you are like a learner driver who travels with headlights blazing and pushes others off the road. When you are a more balanced Christian, you dip your lights in recognition that Christ brings us to heaven via several different routes, and you give other cars space. But when you've been a Christian for a long time, sometimes your battery gets a bit flat and you drive on sidelights, so that you no longer encourage others on the road to the Kingdom of God.'

'Look up at the heavens and count the stars – if indeed you can count them … So shall your offspring be.'

Genesis 15:5

---

1. David Rhodes, *Lenten Adventure* (London: SPCK Publishing, 2000).

34.
Never look back

I OCCASIONALLY wished that my father had been a county cricketer, or an international golfer or a sports commentator.

Whatever he did in that line, he would have been famous and rich. Instead, he chose the harder role and served others as a minister.

He was not particularly clever; writing sermons was a chore. There were some people in his churches whose narrow or bigoted attitudes distressed him. Inherited manse gardens, mostly unkempt, were a constant struggle to maintain. His income was pitiful but he never looked back with regret.

He used his sportsmanship unselfishly, to teach children or convince sceptics that Christianity could be intermixed with worldly things by being a good loser, or encouraging one's opponent.

In the end, he brought more intense, personal joy to a far greater number of people than could ever have benefited from watching him hit a long drive at St Andrew's or a six at Lords.

When a former vicar of mine preached about tithing and putting the Kingdom of God first, he set a shining example. He had adapted his Cambridge-trained mind to preach to a congregation of which many were poorly educated. He had given up a barrister's salary to join the Church. Yet he was truly happy.

How often do we choose the easy option for ourselves, or for our children? Choosing the job which brings in the most money or the one where we don't have to think too hard – instead of asking what God really wants us to do?

And when He has told us, it is vital not to look back: to dwell on the luxuries we might have had, the partner we might have married, or the directorship we just missed. We simply have to trust that, however great the sacrifice seems at the time, the end result will be for our good – and for the greater good of others.

Jesus replied, 'No-one who puts his hand to the plough and looks back is fit for service in the kingdom of God.'
Luke 9:62

35.
Perfect hospitality

SIR Walter Scott was renowned for his hospitality at Abbotsford, his stately home near Melrose in Scotland, and his two great-great-great-granddaughters inherited this fine trait.

Mrs Patricia Maxwell-Scott and Miss (later, Dame) Jean Maxwell-Scott introduced their staff and friends to us incomers during the Historic Houses Festival in 1976, and gave us a splendid buffet supper in the dining room overlooking the River Tweed, where Sir Walter spent his final hours in 1832.

Afterwards we moved to the spacious library for a concert of Border songs and narrative, including the original tune of *My Name is Little Jock Elliott*, which had been lost for 150 years until recently discovered on Mull by musicologist Francis Collinson.

I asked permission to do a write-up of the evening for a Scottish magazine, and this was instantly granted. Having been fascinated by all Sir Walter's memorabilia (including Napoleon's wartime travelling desk), I was taken to see a copy of Victorian actor Garrick's bed before a welcome coffee in the kitchen. It was late when I left, but Jean came out with their West Highland

White, Corrie, and waved a large white handkerchief.

The following day, I visited Francis Collinson and his wife at Innerleithen – on the recommendation of Patricia, to help me with the dialect of some of the Scottish tunes. He and Elizabeth lived in a charming white house with a turret which once belonged to Princess Beatrix, the dear little Mousedene burn burbling nearby. I was treated to a delicious homemade tea and courteously given answers to all my questions.

St Columba's Rune of Hospitality reads:

I saw a stranger yestreen:
I put food in the eatingplace
Drink in the drinking-place …
Often, often, often comes the Christ
In the stranger's guise.

Hebrews 13:2 echoes this:

Do not forget to entertain strangers, for by so doing some people have entertained angels without knowing it.

36.
Prodigal turned pilgrim

BETWEEN March and November 1990, Bill Irwin became the first blind person to walk the length of the 2,167-mile Appalachian Trail from Georgia to Maine, in the USA.

With him was his guide dog Orient, a faithful Alsatian, who carried his own pack. They climbed hazardous mountains, waded through freezing rivers and suffered extremes of temperature. Bill had struggled with many years of alcoholism, but at fifty-two years old was celebrating the third anniversary of his sobriety. He had also been a heavy smoker, gone through four divorces and been estranged from his children until he became a Christian.

Every day on the trail, Bill realised his promise to God, to himself and the multitude who read his story in their newspapers or watched him interviewed on TV. Several times he escaped death, as well as coping with a bear and an army of field mice. He also suffered from broken ribs and very many falls.

His Sunday school class in Burlington prayed for him and Orient every week during his hike. He believed that God listens to His children's prayers and responds to them. Bill did not understand why he had been stuck in a fire warden's cabin surrounded by deep snow for three days, but he knew God wanted to keep him humble and thankful.

'I guess the Lord put me on the Trail with my blindness to let other people see what He could do. My job was to show up for work every day and walk as far as He gave me strength to walk. God needed a weak man for that job, somebody who had to depend on Him for every step.'[1]

'I will set out and go back to my father ...'

Luke 15:18

---

1. Bill Irwin and David McCasland, *Blind Courage* (London: Hodder & Stoughton, 1993).

37.
Rainbow marked the start of new life

Walk on a rainbow trail of song, and all about you will be beauty. There is a way out of every dark mist, over the rainbow trail.

Song of the Navajo Indian

THIS is the story of Terry – formerly a footballer and ambulance driver. 'In 1986 I was informed by a consultant that I was suffering from cancer of the left kidney. That was successfully removed a few weeks later and everything in my life seemed wonderful. In 1988 I had cancer in my remaining kidney. The second surgery was much more traumatic, almost ended my life, and left me with just half a kidney.

'A few days after the second surgery, as I lay in my hospital bed, I realised that it was Maundy Thursday. I looked out on a clear blue sky and determined that I would never get out of my bed again, unless I did it then. I dragged myself and my attachments to the window and saw the Winchester valley bathed in glorious sunshine and the Easton daffodil fields in full bloom.

'Suddenly black clouds heralded a thunderstorm;

but after fifteen minutes the sunshine returned and a beautiful rainbow appeared above the spire of Christ Church. I realised then that God was telling me something; maybe I was being prepared to meet Him. I stood in awe and wept. Collapsing back on to my bed in total confusion, was this the end, I wondered?

'In fact, it was just the beginning, as from then on I started to recover and within a week was home again. Some six months later I was confirmed at Christ Church, and now attend there regularly. I was not aware at the time, of course, that there had been many church members praying for me while I was in hospital. How wonderful is the power of the Lord!'

During an event at Winchester Baptist Church in June 2006, Terry was interviewed and stated: 'Every day is a bonus.'

Tests in 2010 revealed that the remaining kidney had grown to two-thirds of its original size. Terry and his wife subsequently planned visits to family in New Zealand and Canada, where they are hoping to see their first great-grandchild.

'Whenever I bring clouds over the earth and the rainbow appears in the clouds, I will remember my covenant between me and you ...'

Genesis 9:14–15

38.
Recalling a gift

MY memory at school was photographic, a wonderful gift for passing examinations.

Like my godfather, the author Angus MacVicar, I also played up and learnt little in the Latin class. But I bought 'cribs' which gave translations, learnt them by heart and was the only Latin student to pass GCE O level in our form.

The English mistress was also a poor disciplinarian. In order to achieve A level, I memorised long passages of Shakespeare and his critics, seeing the printed page in my mind's eye.

Over the years, my memory suffered quite a battering, and was often hazy. I tried memory books without success, but was somewhat encouraged by those over fifty who said they could not remember things either.

However, God had not given up on me. A few years ago I attended a church in the countryside on the Sunday after Easter. An archdeacon recounted the riveting story of a Red Cross worker imprisoned in Singapore. Some of the facts I remembered, and the following Easter I phoned him to ask for a full account. (See 'A symbol of hope in jail', p.22.)

It was seven years since I last wrote in shorthand. I thought it would be impossible to use it now, so started in longhand; but that proved too slow. After a moment's relaxation, like a miracle my shorthand came back – every word! I transcribed it straight away except for one outline. Three hundred words were prescribed for the article I was writing. The Archdeacon thought he had dictated far too many, but 285 words was the total and I needed a few in hand for the Bible quote. How gracious is the Lord!

In 2005, I attended a healing service at Christ Church, Winchester, and received prayer for a bad back and insomnia. Instead, God granted restoration of my long-distance sight, lapsed charismatic tongue, soprano singing voice *and* my memory!

Satisfy us in the morning with your unfailing love …
Make us glad for as many days as you have afflicted us …
Psalm 90:14–15

39.
Retaliation is not the answer

IN 2001 I was watching a film about Admiral Nelson and Emma Hamilton, when the news of the 9/11 terrorist attack on America broke in. Immediately I thought: 'The Apocalypse has arrived.'

The crumbling upper storeys of the World Trade Center, the fourth highest building in the world, where I myself had climbed to the top in the 1970s and from where cars down below looked like Dinky Toys, were reduced to smoking rubble, and thousands of innocent people were killed.

For some time Christians have thought the world is coming to an end, and have prophesied the return of Jesus soon. Where was God in all this horror? Why such suffering?

Jesus said on the cross, 'My God, my God, why have you forsaken me?' (Matthew 27:46). And in the Garden of Gethsemane He had begged God, His Father, to remove the cup of suffering, to no avail. God had a bigger plan: for Jesus to become the Saviour of the world by over-coming death and rising again, so that He could live in each one of us if we want Him.

If Jesus really lives in us, we can spread the good news of God's Kingdom by the love we show to others, and the world will be a safer place. All we have to do is repent of our sins and believe in Jesus.

Having done this, we become Christians and are born again. We want to behave differently and our values are different, so retaliation is not the right response, however tempting; and I myself have sometimes yielded.

'... be earnest, and repent. Here I am! I stand at the door and knock. If anyone hears my voice and opens the door, I will come in and eat with him, and he with me.
To him who overcomes, I will give the right to sit with me on my throne, just as I overcame and sat down with my Father on his throne.'

Revelation 3:19–21

40.
Saluting the bravery
of our seafarers

MY friend and I once took a waterbus cruise around
Portsmouth Harbour, Hampshire and saw the
second *Ark Royal*, which was launched by the Queen
Mother shortly before she died.

Admiral Horatio Nelson was without doubt Britain's
greatest seaman, and died in action aboard his ship,
HMS Victory, killed by a French sniper in 1805. His body
was stowed in a barrel of brandy to preserve it until his
funeral in St Paul's Cathedral, London. He was wrapped
in the Admiral's and jack flags, but his sailors tore the
ensign flag into strips as mementoes. One of these,
enframed in oak from *HMS Victory*, hangs in Portsmouth
Anglican Cathedral.

Also in the cathedral is the grave of a representative
crew member from the *Mary Rose*, which sank on 19 July
1545 and carried 400 fighting men plus the crew, making
it overladen. The hull was recovered in October 1982.
We watched the Archdeacon of the Isle of Wight leading
a children's service. It was good to think that part of
this building, begun in 1185 as a church for masses

to be sung for the murdered St Thomas à Becket of Canterbury, was still being used during the week to teach youngsters the love of Jesus.

Near the Royal Garrison Church is a beautiful epitaph to the servicemen of Portsmouth who fell between 1914 and 1918, 'holding high for future generations the great standard of duty and the divine law of sacrifice … Their imperishable deeds, unsurpassed in the history of the world, are enshrined forever in the heart of their country … Also … prisoners of war [who] faced with unbroken spirit and unconquerable courage, unspeakable sufferings and privations … We know they have passed from death to life.'

Others went out on the sea in ships; they were merchants on the mighty waters.

Psalm 107:23

41.
When God does not seem to answer

'FREEDOM from worry comes from the surrender of all our rights and all our loved ones to God,' quoted Justyn Rees in *Honest Doubt, Real Faith*.[1] Justyn inherited Hildenborough Hall Christian Centre in Kent but, after bringing many young people to Jesus through his preaching, he had to close the centre because of his subsequent lack of faith.

He had prayed and read encouraging Bible quotes in search of a home for himself and family, a staff house, and complete healing for his cousin Max Sinclair after his car accident – to find none of these things materialised when and how he wished.

After months of depression spent alone on the Hebridean island of Skye and with his family touring America, he heard in a church in San Diego that repressed anger led to bitterness, then depression and doubt. He concluded: 'You can recognise genuine faith not so much by a person's ability to work miracles as by his willingness to obey. The greatest thing I have learned is that I am safe in God's faithfulness.'

Justyn bought an old vicarage in Shoreham where John Wesley had stayed and taught. Wesley also went through a time of depression after failure as a missionary in America; until another missionary preacher in Oxford told him to 'Preach faith till you have it; and then because you have it, you will preach faith.'

Despite partial paralysis, Max Sinclair became a popular speaker; he also published several books. The staff house, which was to be partly paid for by a rich widow who then opted out, sold at nearly twice the original purchase price, and the surplus covered the time when Hildenborough was closed.

Justyn recovered his faith and preached to thousands in Westminster Central Hall and the Royal Albert Hall, London.

I myself have suffered intermittently from Bipolar Disorder (manic depression) from the age of eighteen to sixty-eight. Medication and therapy have helped considerably, but the faithful prayers of many and a growing awareness of Christ's love have proved the ultimate answer.

Jesus said:

'Trust in God; trust also in me.'

John 14:1

---

1. Justyn Rees, *Honest Doubt, Real Faith* (London: Hodder & Stoughton, 1999).

42.
Search hard for the best in life

'THE Forest will always be there … and anybody who is Friendly with Bears can find it,' wrote A.A. Milne.[1] But, like forests, the best things in life are often neglected. To find them, we need to search hard. Brambles may prick and try to deter us, but the secret glades which gave delight in childhood are only rediscovered by those adults who are doughty scramblers. Sometimes the way in is so close that we can easily miss it.

A blind old lady repeatedly asked a young woman to choose a keepsake from her infinitesimal stock of worldly goods. Yet every picture or vase was spoken for.

After the old lady's death, the woman begged her friends for some memento of the thirty years' friendship. All that remained was sent to her: a small cardboard box full of letters and cards; but in her disappointment, she didn't even bother to read them.

During a spring-clean, several years later, the box was an obvious target. One letter after another – including many she had written while away working in Edinburgh – and the old lady's nursing certificates went into the wastepaper basket.

Suddenly, the woman's heart nearly stopped beating from excitement. There, near the bottom of the pile, was a letter dated 1928 from her grandmother and another from her father – both thanking this school Sister for her affectionate care.

The father's letter, written just after he had left boarding school, described in detail the challenge and happiness of working for a mission among the slum dwellers in Manchester.

The young woman treasured these letters far above any material gift the school Sister could have given her. She realised, too, that it was *she* who had been blind. How glad she felt to have finally held back the thorns and glimpsed the Enchanted Places!

God's laws ... are more desirable than gold.
Psalm 19:9–10 (TLB)

---

1. A.A. Milne, *The House at Pooh Corner* (London: Methuen & Co. Ltd, 1949), p.x.

43.
So much joy from nature

DO you get a thrill whenever you see one of your favourite flowers in bloom? I do, and I'm not ashamed at gazing into people's gardens or sniffing shrubs that overhang the pavement. My cousin Judith laughed at me because when we went to Mottisfont Rose Garden near Romsey in June, I always knelt down to smell the pinks!

When I was at prep school in Somerset, a teacher told us where to find wild cowslips in profusion on chalky soil; also the habitat of bee- and butterfly-orchids. One summer holiday, our headmistress set us the task of collecting, pressing and labelling wild flowers in colour groups. Sadly, children would not be allowed to do this today.

In April 2001, I went for a walk round my residential area of Winchester. Marsh marigolds glowed in a pond, magnolias were etched against an orange sunset, brilliant blue grape hyacinths stood on a bank, and masses of wild primroses filled garden borders. A single fritillary hung its spotted head in an otherwise uninteresting plot.

I am always excited at seeing fritillaries since a porter

at Magdalen College, Oxford told me of the legend of St Frideswide. He said: 'She was a very holy woman and wherever she went, fritillaries sprang up behind her. There is a field full of them in our grounds near the River Cherwell. They come up during the first week or so of April and botanists visit us from all over Europe.'

Another story is told that upright fritillaries bordered the road to Calvary. When Jesus passed with His cross, they bowed their heads. And if you shake them, tears will fall.

'See how the lilies of the field grow … Yet … not even Solomon in all his splendour was dressed like one of these.'
Matthew 6:28–29

Our life is a garden

We are flowers planted out
By our Maker's hand:
Some of us in bright sunshine,
Some in shadowland.

Each is different and unique,
All respond to care,
Giving joy to those who seek
Love and beauty rare.

Gardens full of gravel bleak,
Paving stones quite bare,
Weeds and unmown grass abound –
Much laziness is there.

But when the sower does his task,
Then God will bless the deed:
So many colours greet the eye,
Fulfilling every need.

Flaming poppies open wide,
Roses share their scent,
Love-in-a-mist reflects the sky,
All are heaven-sent.

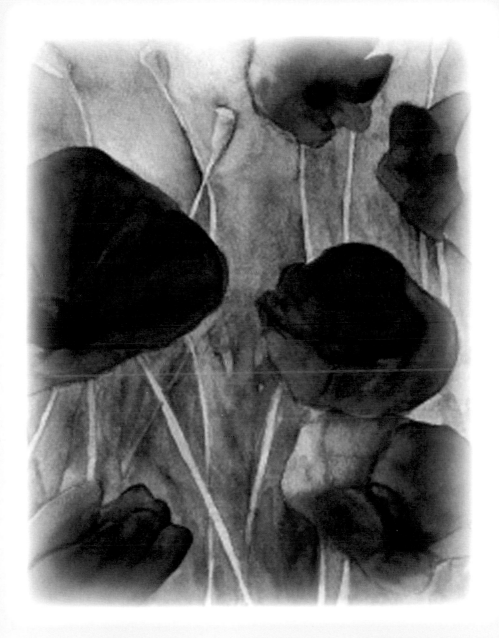

44.
Sowing the seeds

AN unknown vicar arrived at the door, with an expression of concern on his face. Rapidly it changed to relief when he saw the half-dozen small packets destined via his luggage for the Holy Land.

'Oh, that's all right. I thought you were going to give me a suitcase of books,' he said.

Little did we then realise that every single packet would be opened by the charming but vigilant El Al customs ladies at Heathrow!

Since the vicar had taken me on trust, he must have been hard put to explain his apparent smuggling and who I was. Fortunately, he had been given gift copies of the contents prior to departure: booklets on Christian meditation which I hoped would sell in Israel's Christian bookshops.

The blind author, Isabel Henderson, had greatly impressed me by her achievement in privately publishing and selling numerous copies with the aid of a Braille note-taking machine, a typewriter which she had never been properly trained to use, and the kind services of a typist. We regularly exchanged tapes, on which I recorded my poems.

If anyone deserved a helping hand, she did.

When the vicar called at St Andrew's Church, Tiberias, the assistant was flustered by the large number of customers; but dutifully he delivered free samples of Isabel's work. In Jerusalem he took them to the Garden Tomb and braved the fortress-like Church of St Andrew – where he was respectfully salaamed by an Arab employee.

Weeks of silence and postal rejection implied failure of the enterprise. Then came an excited phone call from Isabel Henderson in Scotland.

'I've had an urgent order for twelve copies of my books from St Andrew's Church, Tiberias. Isn't it wonderful to think of them selling beside the Sea of Galilee?' A postcard from St Andrew's, Jerusalem followed – expressing admiration of Isabel's faith. The seeds were beginning to germinate at last!

It was not until I phoned to thank the vicar that I discovered his trial at Heathrow and that he was in the midst of writing a biography of a missionary who braved the deserts of Ethiopia.

'Still other seed fell on good soil, where it produced a crop …'

Matthew 13:8

45.
Voicing a host of happy memories

FROM the age of three to thirteen, I attended Sunday services at a Methodist boys' school where my father was its first chaplain.

Hymn-singing was a rousing affair, and two of my favourites were 'Guide me O Thou Great Redeemer' and 'The day Thou gavest, Lord, is ended'.

The complete usurpation of hymns in some churches by songs and choruses is disappointing. They lack poetry and inspiration to learn them by heart, although they can be quite moving. Surely we need both?

At school I sang in Handel's *Messiah* annually; and while working in Oxford, joined the Oxford Bach Choir. We performed such masterpieces as Verdi's *Requiem*, Elgar's *The Dream of Gerontius* and Handel's *Israel in Egypt*.

Sometimes I practised aloud in the flat I shared with a friend who was not musical. Once, when I got home, she asked me to stand outside the bathroom where she was having a bath. The landing wall ajoined that of the next-door neighbours.

'Now, Joy, sing that chorus: "He sent them hailstones for fire".'

After a bit, she called out: 'That will do. The neighbours' dogs have been barking for ages, so your singing is fair reprisal!'

In London, I became a member of the London Philharmonic Choir. The most uplifting concert in which I ever sang was Bach's *Saint Matthew Passion* at the Royal Festival Hall. We were coached by Freddy Jackson of the Royal Academy of Music, and then Karl Richter from Munich took the final rehearsal and the performance itself.

He played the harpsichord continuo as well as conducting, and drew from us singers every ounce of musicianship we could muster. There was no other conductor equal to him.

At the end, he held up his hand for silence from the audience and crept off the stage.

Speak to one another with psalms, hymns and spiritual songs.

Ephesians 5:19

46.
Tune in to music's healing power

IONCE attended a concert by the Winchester Symphony Orchestra, conducted by Hilary Brooks and featuring Tchaikovsky's 'Violin Concerto', superbly played by Oliver Nelson.

'The Five' Russian composers who succeeded Glinka after his death in 1857 never accepted Tchaikovsky because they judged him too European in his style of composition. Yet his music had what much of theirs lacked: 'a sweet, inexhaustible, supersensuous fund of melody', wrote Fannie Leigh in the programme notes. 'The music often reflected the man – nervous, hypochondriacal and unhappy, with a dark side to his life of which he lived in fear.'

Tchaikovsky wrote his stirring 'Violin Concerto' after a broken nine-week marriage and a nervous breakdown. He took only two months to compose the work, while convalescing in Switzerland in 1878.

The first soloist to receive the composition said it was 'unplayable', and swiftly returned it, but Tchaikovsky did not lose heart. In fact, the second soloist helped make the concerto gradually acceptable to other players, until it achieved the wide popularity of today.

Tchaikovsky's triumph over adversity reminded me of the Rev Dr Selwyn Hughes, who lost his wife through cancer, his two sons through illness; and he himself suffered from cancer, resulting in his death in 2006. Nevertheless, he pressed on in his writing, preaching and teaching ministry as long as he was physically able. The best solution when coping with painful occurrences in life, Selwyn advised, is to use them to aid others who are also hurting. This is what Tchaikovsky did. I went to that concert feeling frazzled and left feeling exhilarated.

Jesus said:

'In this world you will have trouble. But take heart! I have overcome the world.'

John 16:33

47.
Staying in control

IN 1946 while Campbeltown lifeboat coxswain Duncan Newlands was rescuing the survivors of the *Byron Darnton* off the island of Sanda, Kintyre, the US captain called out that four of his crew were still aboard the disintegrating ship fetching a case of whisky 'for your magnificent crew'.

Duncan feared having too many coxswains aboard as a result of drink. He shouted to them not to drop the case into the lifeboat because this might damage her, but to drop it into the water. He then pretended to catch the case with a boathook, but surreptitiously nudged it hard against the ship's side until it broke and sank.

One winter, the author Angus MacVicar was driving Duncan from Glasgow to Campbeltown – a three-hour journey along a difficult, narrow road. It was snowing, and Duncan asked, 'Angus, do you think we should heave to?' 'No, Duncan, I'm the coxswain of this car, and we'll keep going!'

Duncan was doing a programme about the Campbeltown lifeboat for BBC radio's *Children's Hour.* Halfway through he moaned, 'Och to hell, my glasses are all steamed up!' The producer, Kathleen Garscadden, remonstrated: 'Oh, Mr Newlands! We will have to start your bit all over again.'

Duncan owned a boat and took parties of visitors to see the island of Davaar, famous for its cave painting of Christ on the cross. A shingle bank from island to beach forms a causeway at ebb tide. The boat was so low in the water that a man walking along the causeway appeared as if on water. A short Glasgow man in the bow was astonished. 'Hey, mister!' he exclaimed to Duncan, 'There's a fella daein' Jesus oot o' a joab!'

In 1978, I took my father to see this painting, and he was greatly moved.

When the disciples saw him walking on the lake, they were terrified.

Matthew 14:26

At sea

Thick mist shrouds the future;
We cannot see Thy face.
We plod on daily upward,
Hoping for Thy grace.

We *will* believe Thy promise
Of love that never fails,
Of courage in the darkest hour,
And death to the foe that assails.

We would not lose our rudder,
Nor in the doldrums lie;
We'll smite the sounding furrows
Until we heaven espy.

So Saviour stay beside us,
Our Captain and our Lord;
Without You we are shipwrecked;
We need Your mighty Word.

48.
The gift of giving

IN 1982, when my father and I were in the Holy Land, we visited Nazareth – where Jesus grew up and learnt the trade of carpentry. I bought a commemorative plate and hung it on the wall at my home in Bristol.

I never wanted to part with the plate; however, a cousin sadly died in her sixties and I wondered what to give her sorrowing sister at the funeral. She had travelled in the Near East and was interested in ceramics … God led me to give her my treasured Nazareth plate.

Twenty years later in celebration of my sixtieth birthday, I was given a handcrafted plate from Bethlehem, but also portraying Jerusalem and Nazareth – far more attractive than the one I had given away. It had been purchased at a Christmas market in Cologne by my courier friend, the late Sue Bowman of Swanage.

The Reverend Canon Caroline Baston, when Rector of All Saints Church, Winchester (now Archdeacon of the Isle of Wight), told me an amazing story on similar lines. By November 1998, the organ needed refurbishing at a cost of £5,000. A Songs of Praise event was held, raising £900. This, together with the collection at a confirmation, increased the sum to £1,050.

A few days later, TV screens showed a hurricane hitting Central America. It was decided their need was greater, and Canon Baston took a cheque for the amount raised to the Post Office to send to the disaster fund. When she got home, there was a cheque for £1,000 in the post from Hampshire County Council. All Saints had applied for a grant for the organ fund about six months before and had forgotten all about it!

'Give, and it will be given to you ... pressed down, shaken together and running over ... For with the measure you use, it will be measured to you.'

Luke 6:38

49.
True friendship

AT a Scottish guesthouse I found this beautiful definition of true friendship: 'A friend is one to whom one may pour out all the contents of one's heart, chaff and grain together, knowing that the gentlest of hands will take and sift them, keeping what is worth keeping and with a breath of kindness blow the rest away' (Anon).

There are some memorable friendships in the Bible: Ruth and her mother-in-law Naomi; David and Jonathan; Martha, Mary and Lazarus – friends of Jesus; and, most important of all, Jesus and His Father.

While I was struggling to make ends meet as a cleaner for four years, having lost my senior secretarial job at Church House, Winchester due to being allergic to computers(!), several cousins and friends gave me 4-star holidays in their homes.

Age need be no barrier. Barbara de Seyssel – my close friend and mentor – was more than thirty years older than me, yet we had delightful chats while riding through the New Forest, stimulating each other's writing and commiserating over many publishers' rejections!

Another valuable friend for over fifty years was my primary-school English teacher, Mary Garrow – a Quaker descended from an Anglican and a Stoic. This made for some interesting discussions. We met annually at her home in Taunton, and prayed for each other daily. Mary never failed to send me a postcard from her exciting rambling holidays abroad.

At a Winchester church in 1991, God brought my dearest friend Jeanette and me together. Though our paths have sometimes diverted to different churches and countries, He has sustained our friendship and fellowship throughout, teaching us that He must be pre-eminent in our lives.

During the winter of 2009, Jeanette sent me a card designed by Jenny Cooper, an artist at Beauty From Ashes – an organisation founded by Jennifer Rees Larcombe. The quotation read: 'I was regretting the past and fearing the future. Suddenly the Lord was speaking: "MY NAME IS **I AM**. When you live in the past, with its mistakes and regrets, it is hard. I AM NOT THERE. When you live in the future, with its problems and fears, it is hard. I AM NOT THERE. WHEN YOU LIVE IN THIS MOMENT IT IS NOT HARD: I AM HERE. MY NAME IS **I AM**."'

A friend loves at all times …

Proverbs 17:17

---

1. *Listen for the Lord* by Helen Mallicoat © 1977. Hallmark Cards Inc, Kansas City, Missouri, USA. Reproduced with Jenny Cooper's permission.

50.
The Word of God in any language

I PAID my first visit to Winchester Cathedral Library in 2002. There are displayed the four volumes of the Winchester Bible, begun by a scribe in 1160, who copied the text of St Jerome's Latin translation from the Hebrew and Greek.

The scribe almost finished his work, but the illumined characters at the start of each chapter are sometimes unfinished. However, these give an insight into the making of medieval illuminated manuscripts. They were designed by travelling craftsmen and are beautifully decorated with gold and blue lapis lazuli. The vellum (calf skin) is of the highest quality.

The grandson of William the Conqueror, Henry of Blois (Bishop of Winchester from 1129–1171) most probably paid for this wonderful Bible. But he died ten years after it was begun and there was not enough money left to complete it.

Walter Oakeshott, warden of Winchester College in the late 1940s, made a detailed study of this Bible. His book, published in 1981, was called *The Two Winchester Bibles* because there are two of them, but no one knows the whereabouts of the other copy.

In the front hall of Trinity Theological College, Bristol, I saw a communion table used by William Tyndale, who was born in Gloucestershire in 1494. Bishop Tunstall of London refused to allow Tyndale to translate a Bible from Greek and Hebrew into English. So Tyndale moved to Europe, and in 1526 produced 6,000 pocket-sized English Bibles. Only one of these is believed to have survived, because Tunstall's spies destroyed all the rest.

Tyndale was arrested in 1555 as a heretic, imprisoned for sixteen months, strangled and burned at the stake at Vilvorde near Brussels. But by his death 27,000 English copies were circulating, and formed the basis of our Authorised Version, which celebrates its 400th anniversary in 2011.

'… my word that goes out from my mouth: It will not return to me empty, but will accomplish what I desire and achieve the purpose for which I sent it.'
Isaiah 55:11

NATIONAL DISTRIBUTORS

UK: (and countries not listed below)

CWR, Waverley Abbey House, Waverley Lane, Farnham, Surrey GU9 8EP.
Tel: (01252) 784700 Outside UK (44) 1252 784700 Email: mail@cwr.org.uk

AUSTRALIA: KI Entertainment, Unit 21 317-321 Woodpark Road, Smithfield, New South Wales 2164. Tel: 1 800 850 777 Fax: 02 9604 3699 Email: sales@kientertainment.com.au

CANADA: David C Cook Distribution Canada, PO Box 98, 55 Woodslee Avenue, Paris, Ontario N3L 3E5. Tel: 1800 263 2664 Email: sandi.swanson@davidccook.ca

GHANA: Challenge Enterprises of Ghana, PO Box 5723, Accra.
Tel: (021) 222437/223249 Fax: (021) 226227 Email: ceg@africaonline.com.gh

HONG KONG: Cross Communications Ltd, 1/F, 562A Nathan Road, Kowloon.
Tel: 2780 1188 Fax: 2770 6229 Email: cross@crosshk.com

INDIA: Crystal Communications, 10-3-18/4/1, East Marredpalli, Secunderabad – 500026, Andhra Pradesh. Tel/Fax: (040) 27737145 Email: crystal_edwj@rediffmail.com

KENYA: Keswick Books and Gifts Ltd, PO Box 10242-00400, Nairobi.
Tel: (254) 20 312639/3870125 Email: keswick@swiftkenya.com

MALAYSIA: Canaanland, No. 25 Jalan PJU 1A/41B, NZX Commercial Centre, Ara Jaya, 47301 Petaling Jaya, Selangor.
Tel: (03) 7885 0540/1/2 Fax: (03) 7885 0545 Email: info@canaanland.com.my

Salvation Book Centre (M) Sdn Bhd, 23 Jalan SS 2/64, 47300 Petaling Jaya, Selangor.
Tel: (03) 78766411/78766797 Fax: (03) 78757066/78756360 Email: info@salvationbookcentre.com

NEW ZEALAND: KI Entertainment, Unit 21 317-321 Woodpark Road, Smithfield, New South Wales 2164, Australia.
Tel: 0 800 850 777 Fax: +612 9604 3699 Email: sales@kientertainment.com.au

NIGERIA: FBFM, Helen Baugh House, 96 St Finbarr's College Road, Akoka, Lagos.
Tel: (01) 7747429/4700218/825775/827264 Email: fbfm_1@yahoo.com

PHILIPPINES: OMF Literature Inc, 776 Boni Avenue, Mandaluyong City.
Tel: (02) 531 2183 Fax: (02) 531 1960 Email: gloadlaon@omflit.com

SINGAPORE: Alby Commercial Enterprises Pte Ltd, 95 Kallang Avenue #04-00, AIS Industrial Building, 339420. Tel: (65) 629 27238 Fax: (65) 629 27235 Email: marketing@alby.com.sg

SOUTH AFRICA: Struik Christian Books, 80 MacKenzie Street, PO Box 1144, Cape Town 8000.
Tel: (021) 462 4360 Fax: (021) 461 3612 Email: info@struikchristianmedia.co.za

SRI LANKA: Christombu Publications (Pvt) Ltd, Bartleet House, 65 Braybrooke Place, Colombo 2. Tel: (9411) 2421073/2447665 Email: dhanad@bartleet.com

USA: David C Cook Distribution Canada, PO Box 98, 55 Woodslee Avenue, Paris, Ontario N3L 3E5, Canada. Tel: 1800 263 2664 Email: sandi.swanson@davidccook.ca

CWR is a Registered Charity - Number 294387

CWR is a Limited Company registered in England - Registration Number 1990308

Courses and seminars

Publishing and new media

Conference facilities

Transforming lives

CWR's vision is to enable people to experience personal transformation through applying God's Word to their lives and relationships.

Our Bible-based training and resources help people around the world to:
• Grow in their walk with God
• Understand and apply Scripture to their lives
• Resource themselves and their church
• Develop pastoral care and counselling skills
• Train for leadership
• Strengthen relationships, marriage and family life and much more.

Our insightful writers provide daily Bible-reading notes and other resources for all ages, and our experienced course designers and presenters have gained an international reputation for excellence and effectiveness.

CWR's Training and Conference Centre in Surrey, England, provides excellent facilities in an idyllic setting – ideal for both learning and spiritual refreshment.

 CWR Applying God's Word
to everyday life and relationships

CWR, Waverley Abbey House,
Waverley Lane, Farnham,
Surrey GU9 8EP, UK

Telephone: **+44 (0)1252 784700**
Email: **info@cwr.org.uk**
Website: **www.cwr.org.uk**

Registered Charity No 294387
Company Registration No 1990308

Simple stories, important truths

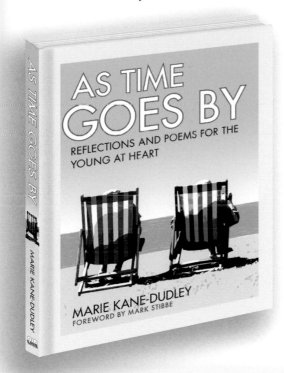

Personal stories, poems, prayers and reflections of an octogenarian, to inspire and uplift those in their 'golden years'.

This 148-page hardback is colour throughout – makes a great gift item!

As Time Goes By
by Marie Kane-Dudley
ISBN: 978-1-85345-487-5

Meet with God through His Word each day

With nearly a million readers worldwide, this daily Bible-reading tool will help you with life's challenges and give you rich insight into the truths of Scripture.

Written by a pastor and counsellor with over 50 years' experience, Selwyn Hughes, and published bimonthly, *Every Day with Jesus* will challenge, inspire, comfort and encourage you in your spiritual walk as you study six topics in depth each year.

Also available in large print format and as a daily email.

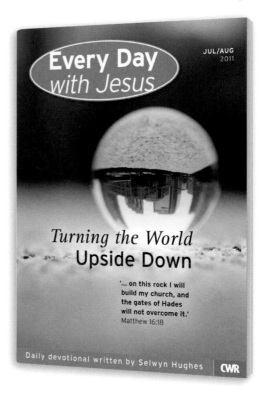

UK Annual Subscription: £14.95 (for six bimonthly issues, incl p&p)
Individual Issues: £2.75 each (plus p&p)
Email Subscription: £13.80 per year

**Order online at www.cwr.org.uk/store
or call 01252 784710 (Mon-Fri, 9.30am-5pm)**

Also available at most Christian bookshops.